MW00450398

"Stride Guitar"

by Guy Van Duser

Online Audio   www.melbay.com/93939

AUDIO CONTENTS

INTRODUCTION

"Stride" was what the post-ragtime style of solo piano playing came to be called, the term itself referring to the pianist's left hand, which moved back and forth between bass and chords, thus providing a complete accompaniment for the right hand improvisations. Much of this piano music can be successfully transcribed for finger-style guitar, with the right hand thumb providing an alternating bass line comparable to the left hand on the piano. The music of "stride" pianists such as James P. Johnson and Fats Waller can offer as much inspiration to guitar players as the piano rags of Scott Joplin. In fact, even the marches of John Phillip Sousa can be adapted to this basic two-beat guitar style!

Some of these arrangements are not easy to play. I hope they will serve to provide a challenge to finger-style guitarists, whether they are hobbyists or performers, and also to encourage more "stride" arrangements by other players as well.

I wish to especially thank Bob Davoli for working through these transcriptions with me, and also John Knowles, who finally got me to write it all down. Thanks also to Chet Atkins for getting excited about my Sousa marches, and to Nikki, who refused to let me give up on the piccolo part.

TABLE OF CONTENTS

THE BOYS OF BLUE HILL

This is the easiest arrangement in this collection, and is basically just a fiddle tune played finger-style in "drop D" tuning. Its smooth, syncopated swing is due to the overlapping effect you get by arranging the melody notes so that successive notes are played on different strings (the way Bill Keith and other players do on banjo). I like to exaggerate the "swinginess" of the tune as I play it.

Incidentally, I've found that it helps to not look at the fingerboard any more than you have to, once you've figured out the notes. Since higher pitches sometimes show up on lower strings, the tune has to be practiced by "feel" until your fingers can remember the way by themselves.

This arrangement is recorded on *The New Pennywhistle Album*, Green Linnet Records, SIF 1013.

THE BOYS OF BLUE HILL

Tune 6th string down to "D":

guitar arrangement
by Guy Van Duser

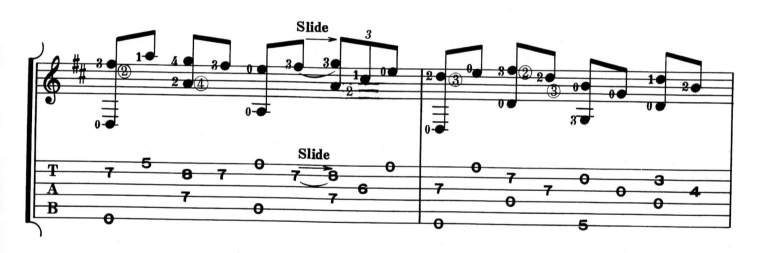

GUITAR BOOGIE SHUFFLE

Practically the first licks anybody ever showed me on guitar were some of the "boogie woogie" bass lines of 50's rock'n roll. I always did love to hear boogie woogie with its driving "eight-to-the-bar" rhythms, but keeping that rolling left hand line going while the right one plays something else entirely has remained beyond my reach, so to speak, on the piano, not that it's any easier to manage on a guitar. However, a guitar can certainly handle properly arranged contrapuntal lines, and working the two halves of the boogie woogie style together comes down to fairly straightforward memorization, line by line. The important thing to work toward in mastering the arrangement is making the treble line sound as spontaneous as possible against the steady progression of the bass. Think of the upper line as a hot Charlie Christian-type solo.

This arrangement appears on *Finger-Style Guitar Solos*, Rounder Records 3021.

"GUITAR BOOGIE SHUFFLE"

**Tune 6th string
to "D":**

Arrangement by
Guy Van Duser

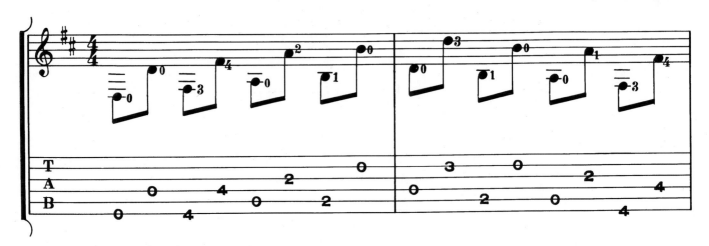

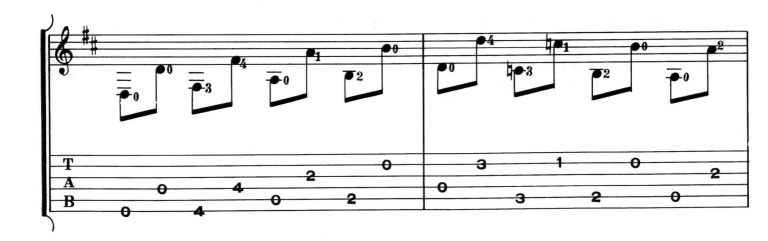

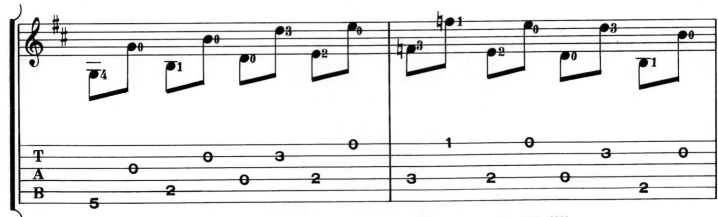

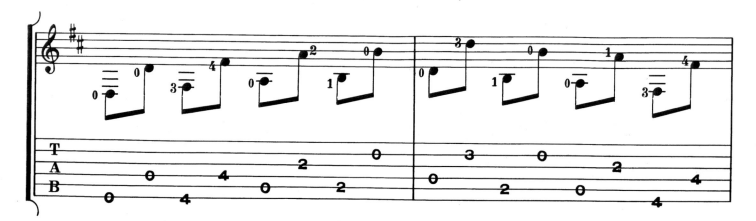

(L.H. Thumb may wrap around neck to play the lower
register notes in these next four measures
opposite 2nd finger, if desired)

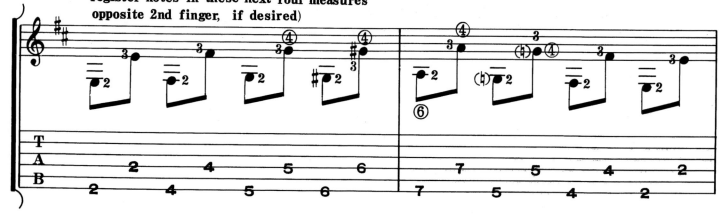

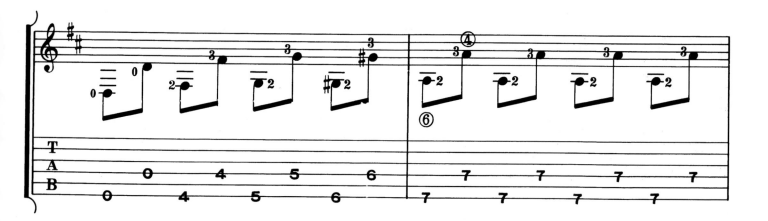

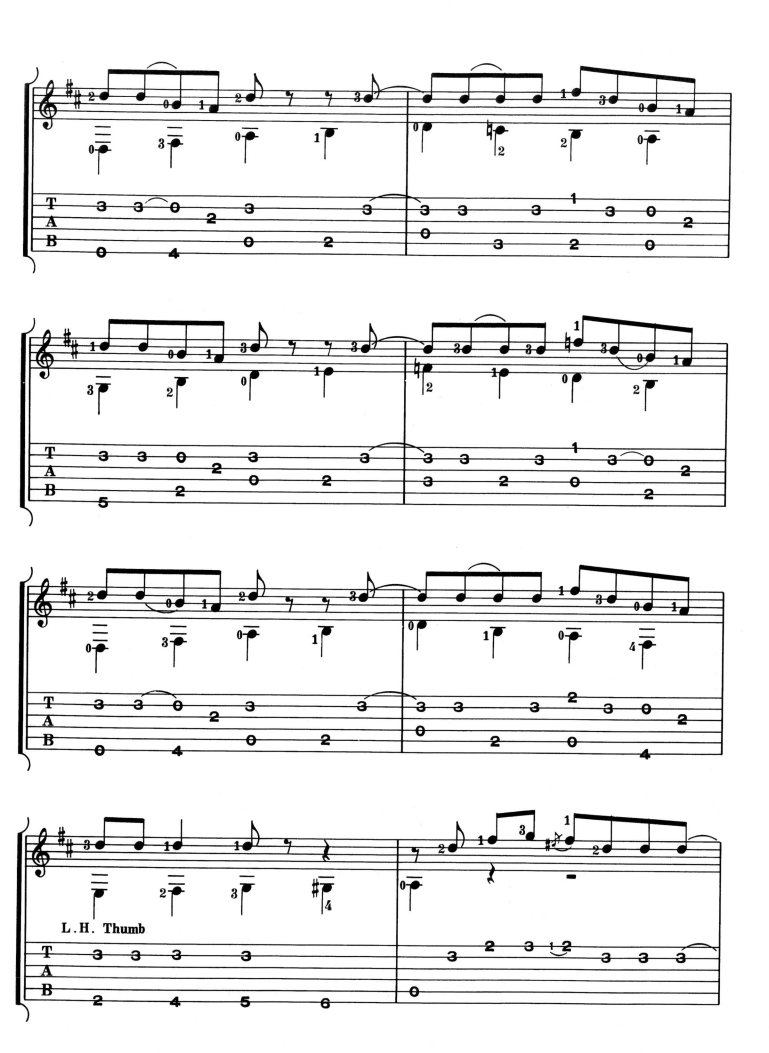

L.H. Thumb

14

CII

ALLIGATOR CRAWL

The "Alligator Crawl" is one of Fats Waller's most famous piano solos, combining stride, boogie woogie, and Fats' own unmistakable style into a jaunty romp at the keyboard. Fitting it onto the fingerboard required lots of room to maneuver, and the boogie woogie line in the bass is again (as in "Guitar Boogie Shuffle") most easily handled in "drop D" tuning. Since the melody seems to stay mostly in the low part of the treble register, I usually play this arrangement capoed at the third fret, raising the key to F.

That long descending set of trills used to change keys for the middle section should be practiced very slowly until it becomes a single reflex; the hand is quicker than the eye!

This tune is recorded on *Stride Guitar*, Rounder Records 3059.

"THE ALLIGATOR CRAWL"

**Tune 6th string
down to "D":**

Thomas "Fats" Waller
arranged for guitar by Guy Van Duser

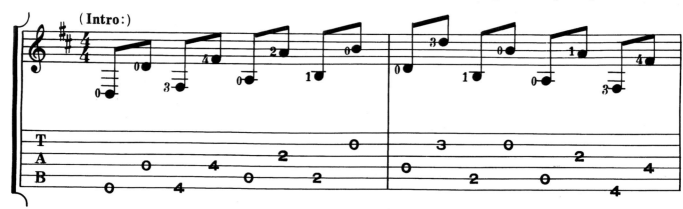

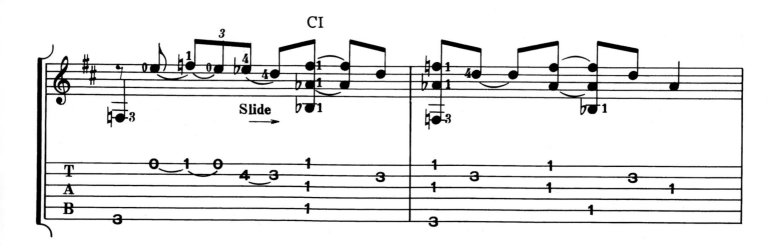

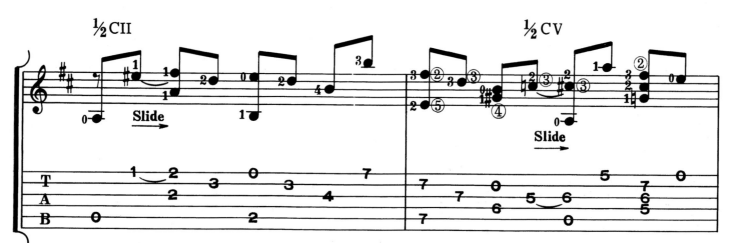

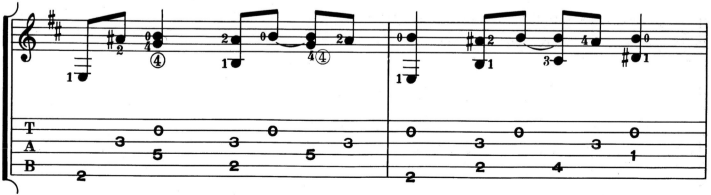

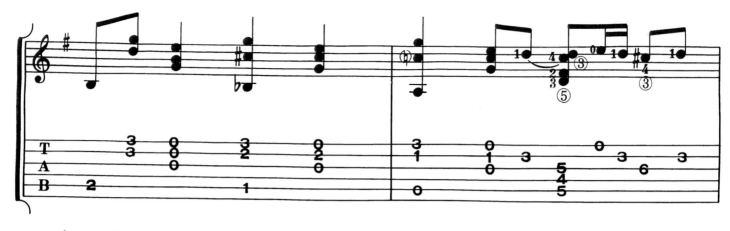

½ CIII ½ CI ½ CIII ½ CI

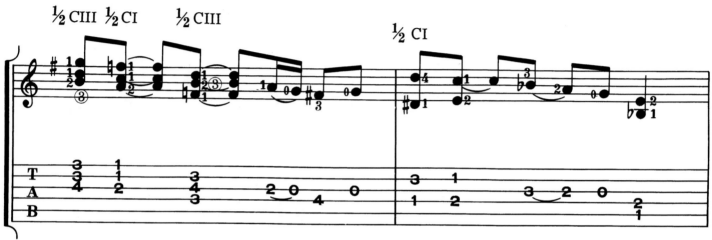

½ CI

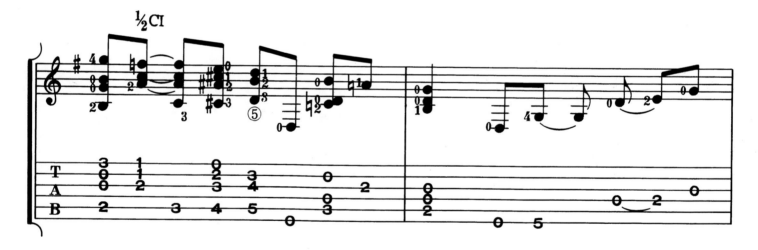

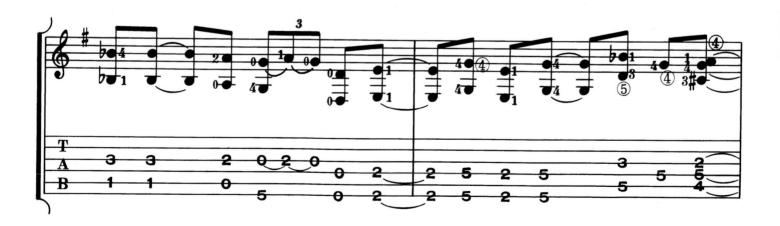

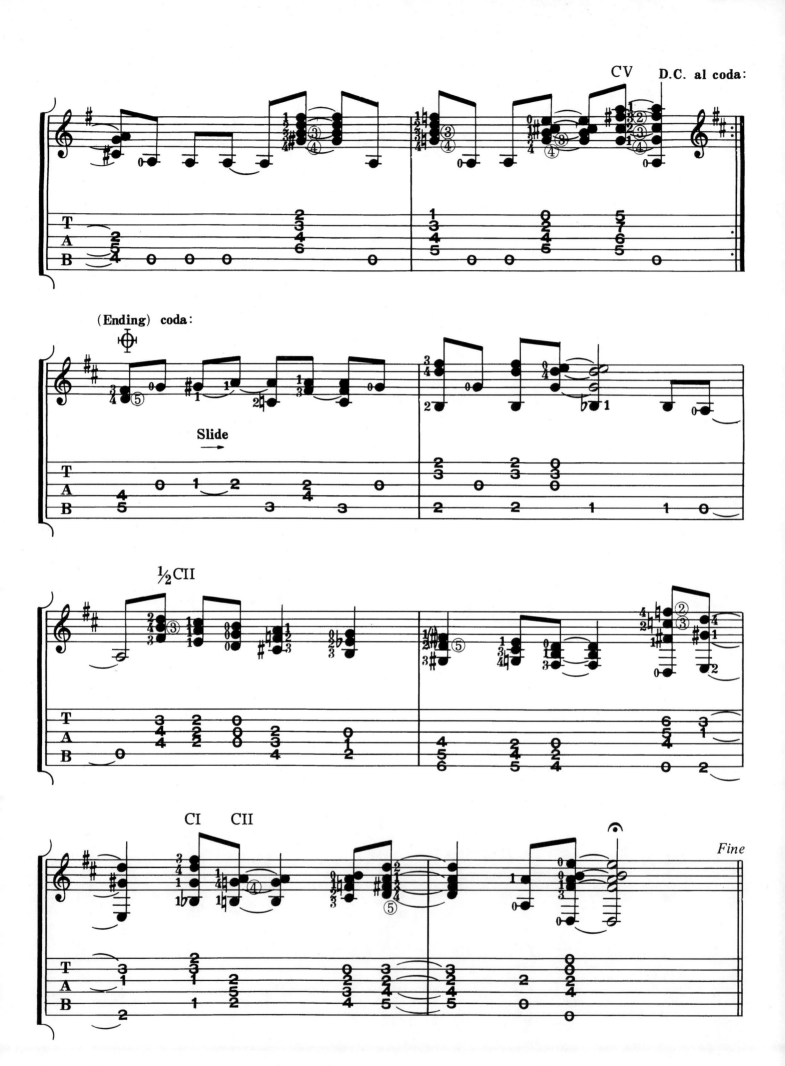

SENECA SLIDE

I wrote this tune after listening very closely to the way Fats Waller plays "broken third" licks on the piano. The lick works by taking the arpeggio of a chord, in this case a major chord, and "displacing" the notes of adjacent thirds, one pair at a time, so that first the lower note is played flat, then the upper note is played sharp, and finally, the pair of notes are sounded together at their correct arpeggio positions. When this lick is played very rapidly, the listener clearly perceives a pattern, but doesn't have time to sort it out (an effect I find to be an ear-pleasing characteristic of many "hot" licks).

Once I had the hang of the lick, I started playing around with different "broken" harmonies, and eventually a few favorite sequences were stitched together into a tune. It's named after one of the Finger Lakes in upper New York State, a favorite vacation spot of mine.

"SENECA SLIDE"

Composed and arranged by
Guy Van Duser

**Tune 6th string
down to "D":**

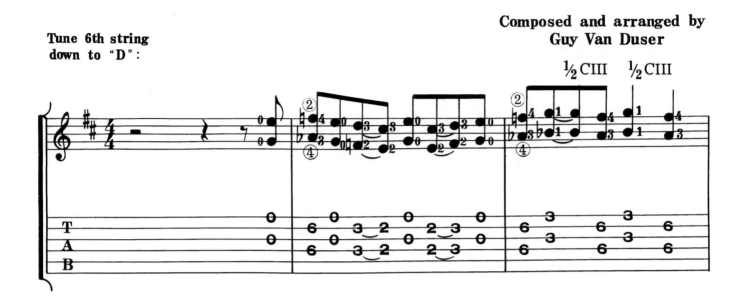

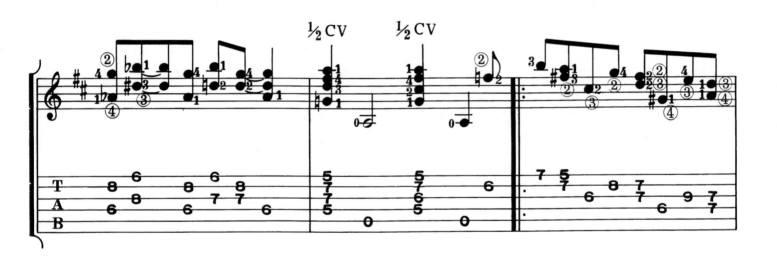

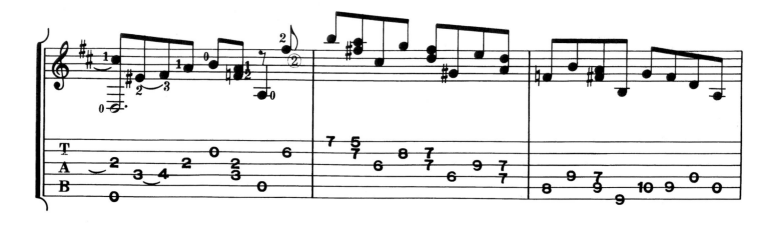

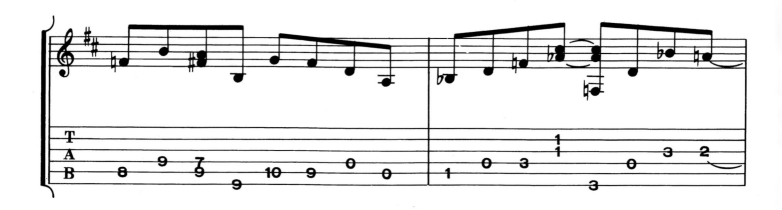

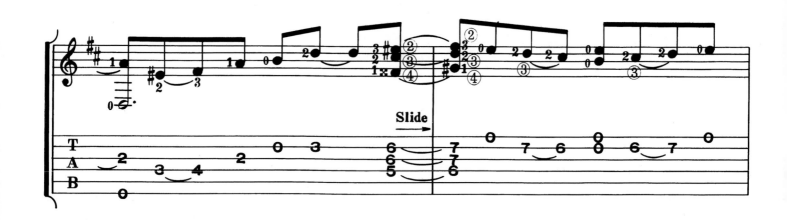

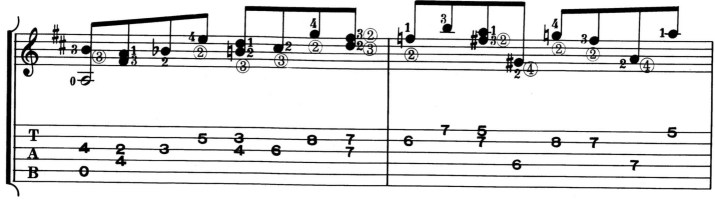

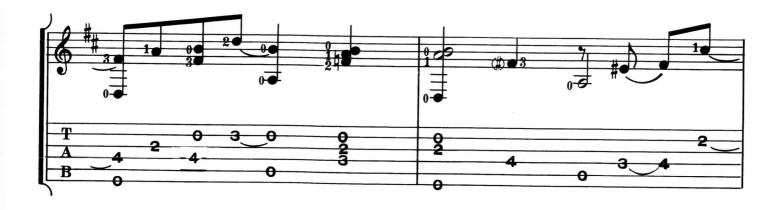

harmonic 7th fret :

1.

harmonic:

harmonic 7th fret

2.

(Repeat of section I:)

½CI

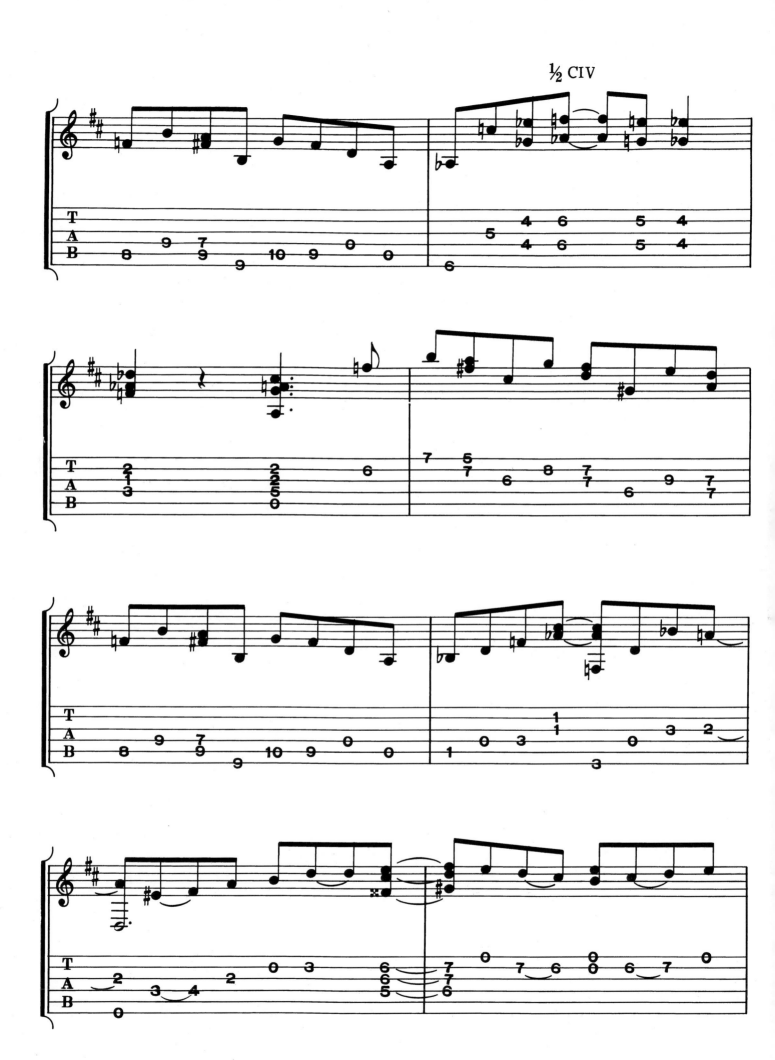

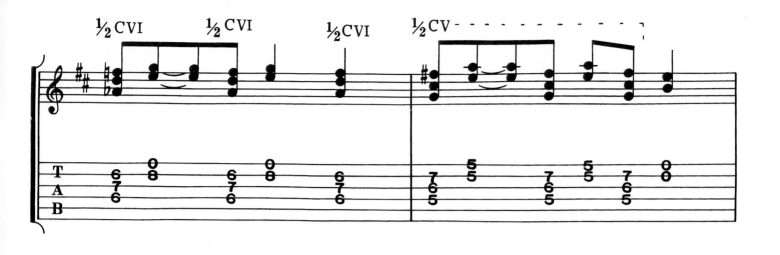

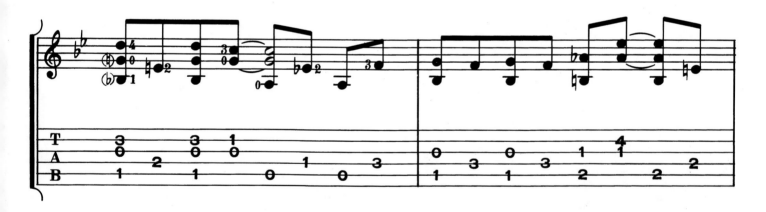

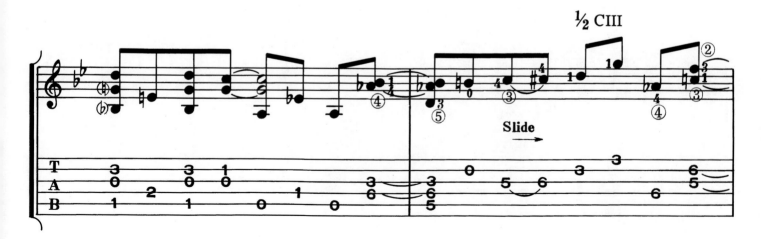

(Final repeat of section I:)

½ CIV

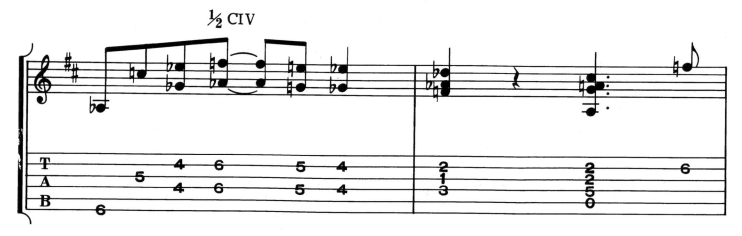

SNOWY MORNING BLUES

James P. Johnson is often called the "father of stride piano". He was an inspiration to many players, such as Fats Waller, and was himself the composer of many classic piano solos in the "stride" style. I found in arranging this tune that it is possible to get closer to the pianist's left hand part than usual. Here, at times, the full stride left hand, a bass tenth interval followed by a chord, can be played on the guitar while still managing the melody on the treble strings. This arrangement is in the original piano key, as well.

It is worth remembering here that the guitar is learning from the piano, rather than merely imitating it. The idea is to expand what can be done on the guitar, while at the same time contributing the sonorities and unique characteristics of the guitar to the interpretation of James P. Johnson's music. For this arrangement I have transcribed only the basic "A" and "B" sections of the tune, in hopes that the reader will go on to assemble his own variations and improvisations, just as the stride pianists inspired each other to do.

This arrangement is performed as a duet with clarinetist Billy Novick on *Stride Guitar*, Rounder Records 3059.

"SNOWY MORNING BLUES"

**Tune 6th string
down to "D":**

James P. Johnson
guitar arrangement
by Guy Van Duser

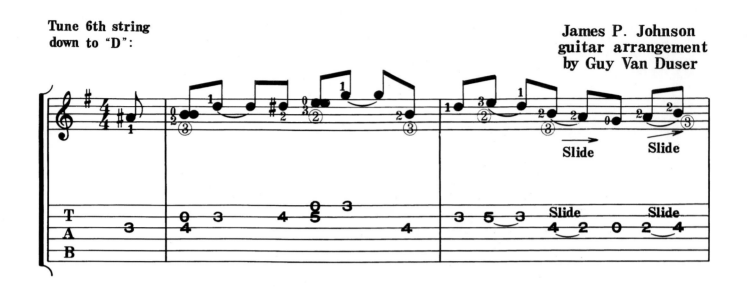

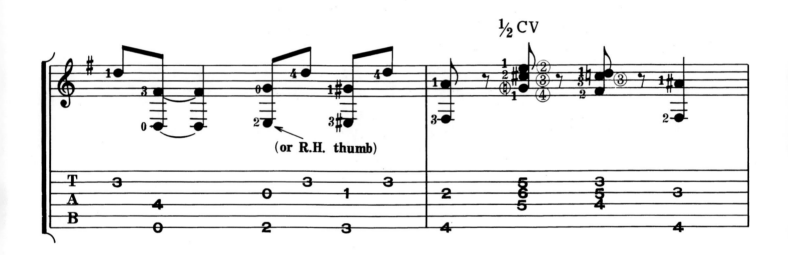

(or R.H. thumb)

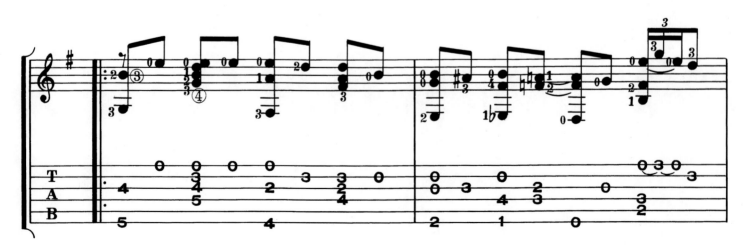

(or R.H. thumb)

½ CII

Slide

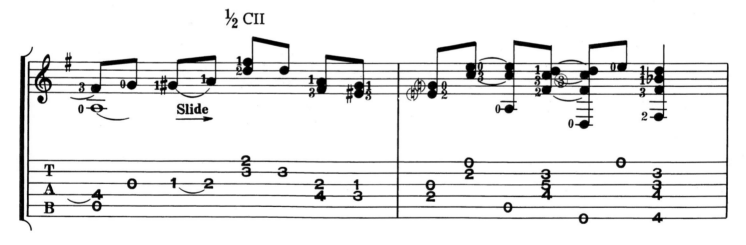

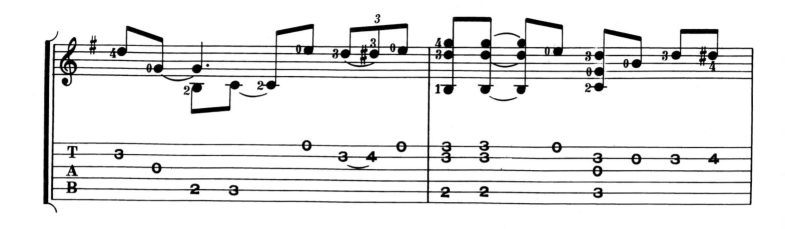

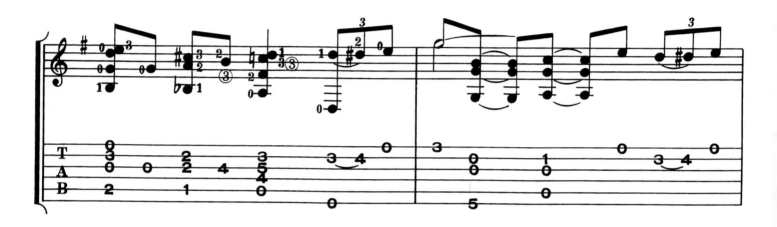

CII - - - - - - - - - -

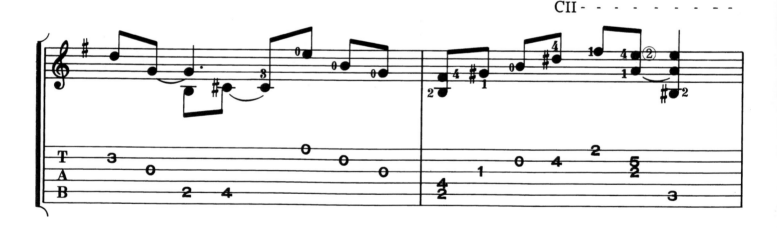

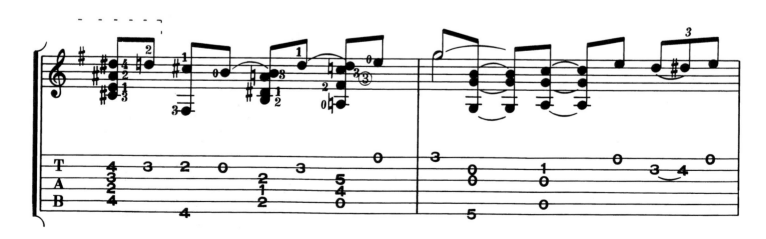

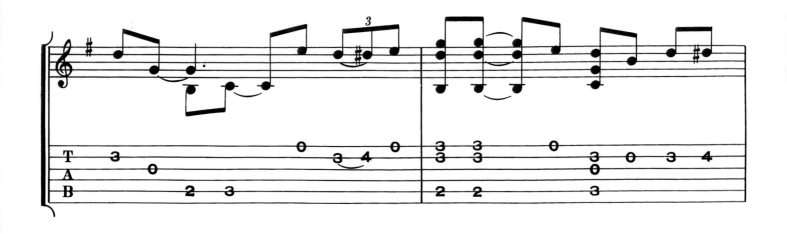

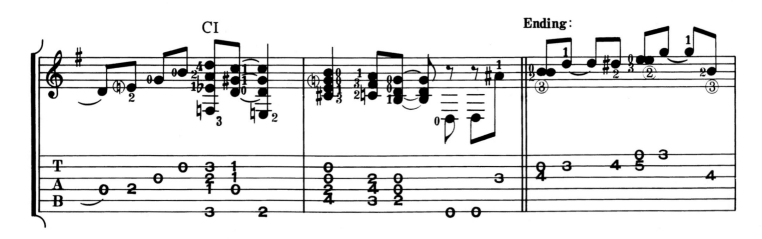

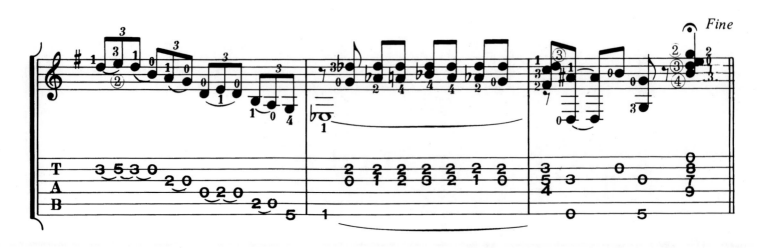

SEMPER FIDELIS

After I had arranged Sousa's "Stars and Stripes Forever" for guitar (that arrangement is presented later on in this book), I tried doing two or three more, including this one, "Semper Fidelis". I came up with an unusual effect in the middle section by borrowing a trick used by flamenco guitarists to imitate the sound of a snare drum. By pulling the sixth string up and over the fifth string and then pinning both strings down in this twisted-over position with the left hand, a snare drum-like sound is produced when these twisted strings are struck together by the right hand. (This trick usually works better on a nylon-string guitar.) In this arrangement I have complicated matters by using the rest of my left hand fingers to play the melody on the treble strings while the drum effect is going on. Your left hand may ache a little bit after this one!

"SEMPER FIDELIS"

John Phillip Sousa
arranged for guitar by Guy Van Duser

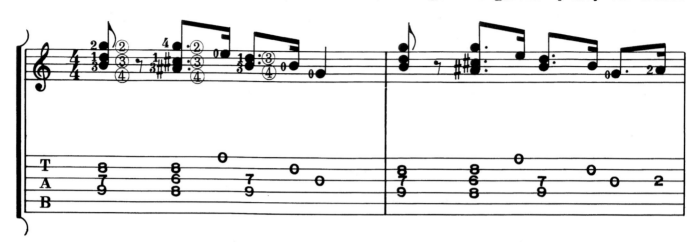

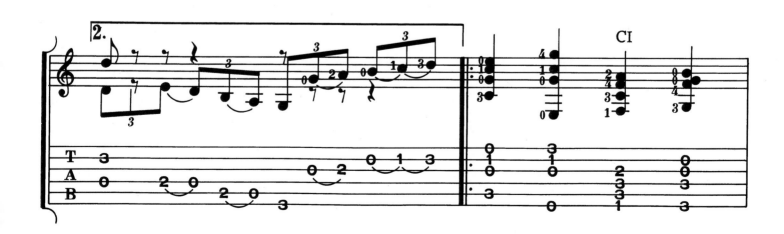

1st finger barre at 5th fret:

Cross 6th string over 5th string and hold with ring finger at 7th fret: Set Snare before taking barre.

(Note "Snare" strings are struck by R.H. Thumb in downstrokes only.)

52

THE STARS AND STRIPES FOREVER

This may be my most-known arrangement; certainly it is the most requested. I figured out this arrangement several years ago, in time for the U.S. Bi-Centennial celebration. I had been playing Scott Joplin rags and wanted to find something different. A Sousa march on guitar seemed like a pretty outrageous idea; it would have lots of energy, plus everybody would be sure to know the tune!

No doubt about it, this one is tough to play! I didn't try to duplicate the complete band arrangement; just playing the various sections finger-style with alternating bass will get the impression of the piece across, and the audience will imagine the rest. The important thing here is to play it like a march, with lots of foot-stomping and pizzazz. Remember, you're an entire marching band!

This arrangement was recorded in front of a live audience for *Finger-style Guitar Solos*, Rounder Records 3021.

P.S. Good luck with the piccolo part!

I sometimes include Stars & Stripes in my show. It is received very well--- Thanks for the arrangement, Guy.

Chet Atkins, CGP

"THE STARS AND STRIPES FOREVER"

Arranged for guitar solo by
Guy Van Duser

John Phillip Sousa

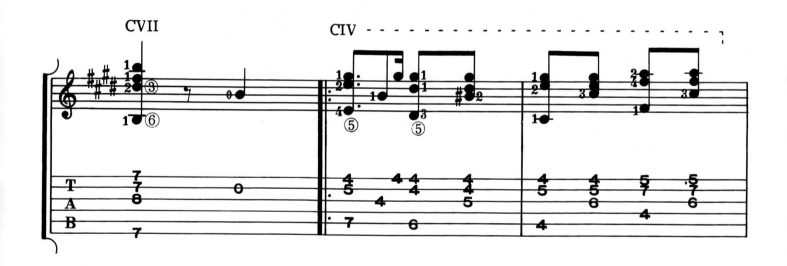

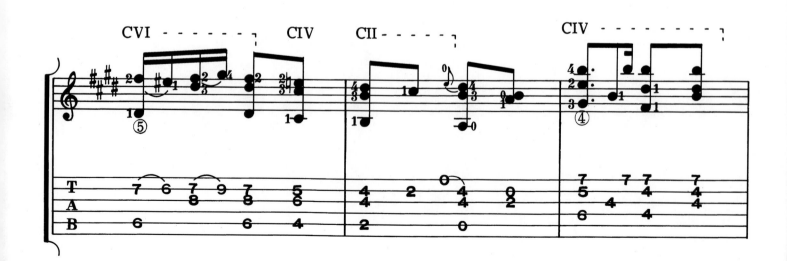

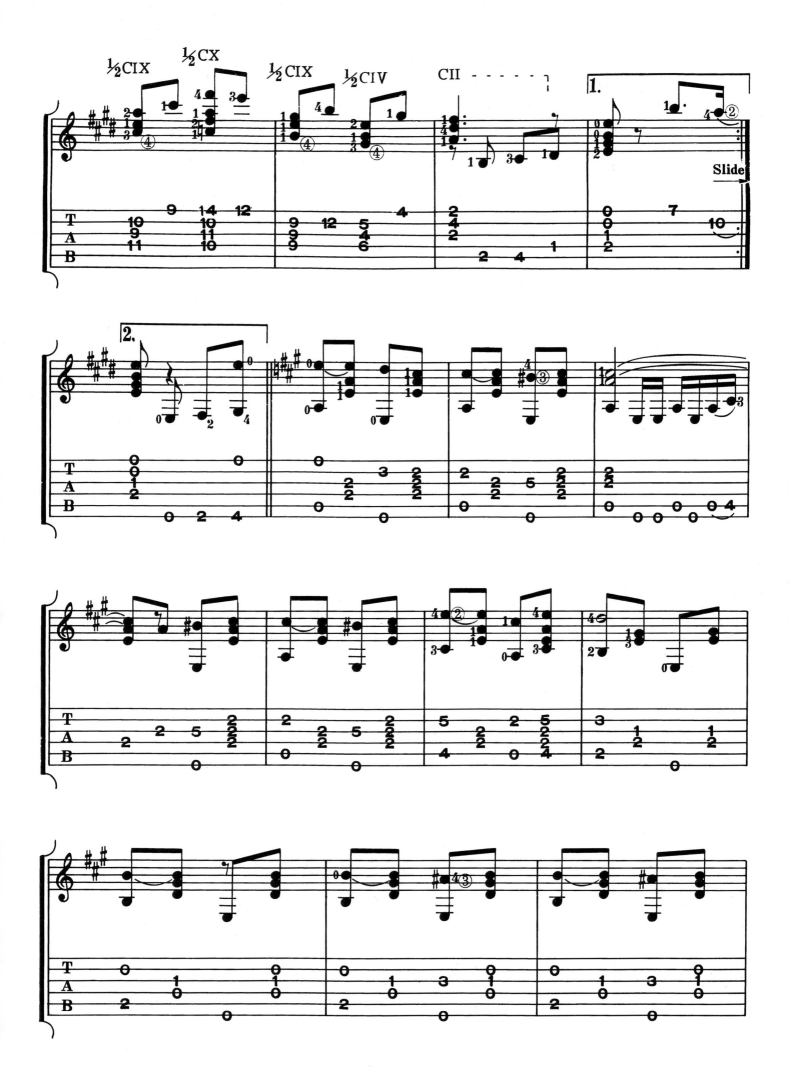

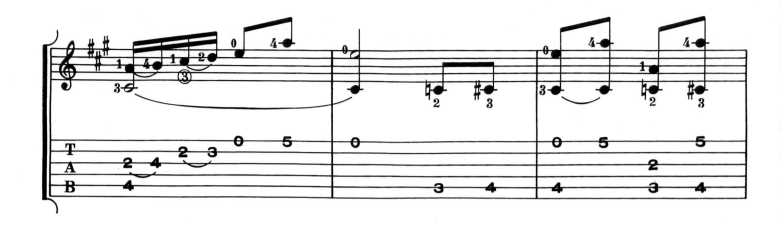

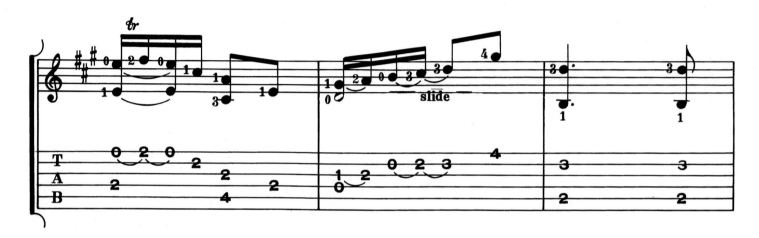

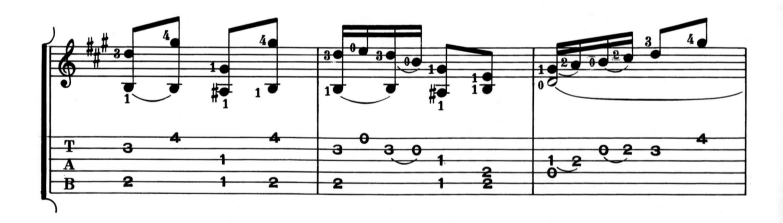

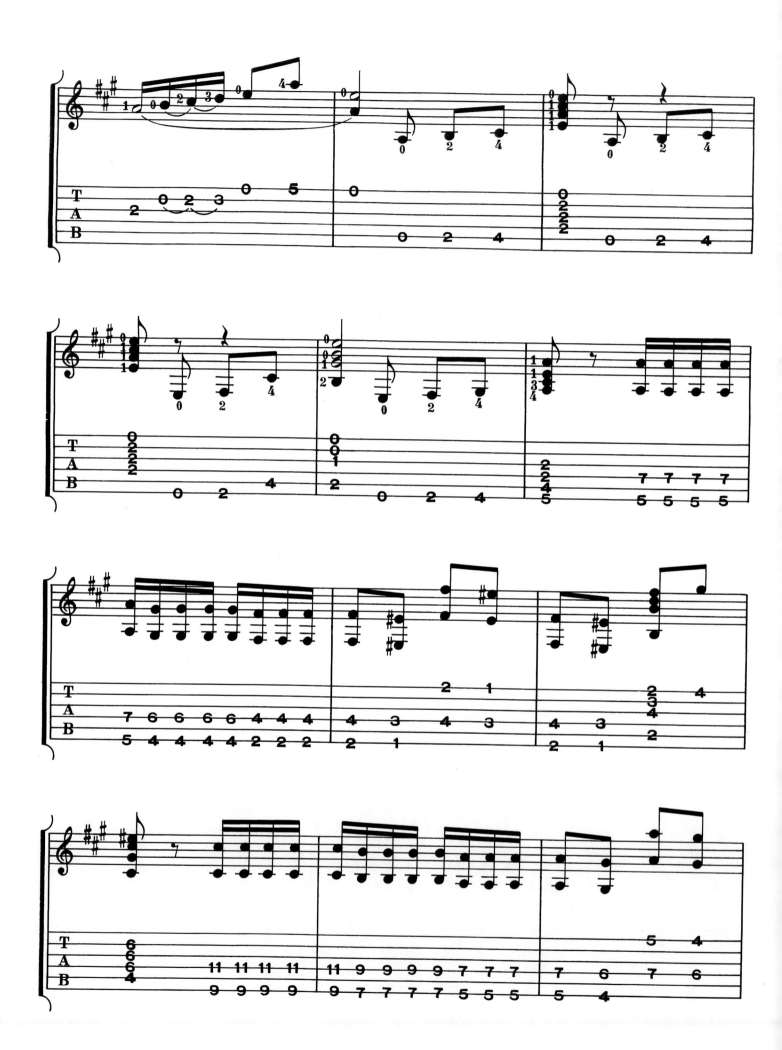

½CII   ½CI

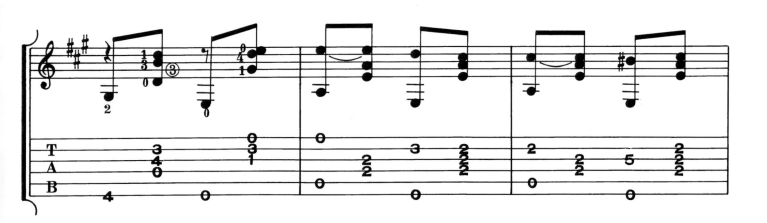

Great Music at Your Fingertips